# A JOURNEY THROUGH LIFE

A Journey Through Life
Copyright © 2024 by Yvonne Bronstorph

Published in the United States of America
ISBN    Paperback:      979-8-89091-488-0
ISBN    eBook:           979-8-89091-489-7

All rights reserved. No part of this publication may be reproduced, stored in a retrieval system or transmitted in any way by any means, electronic, mechanical, photocopy, recording or otherwise without the prior permission of the author except as provided by USA copyright law.

The opinions expressed by the author are not necessarily those of ReadersMagnet, LLC.

ReadersMagnet, LLC 10620 Treena Street, Suite 230 | San Diego, California, 92131 USA
1.619. 354. 2643 | www.readersmagnet.com

Book design copyright © 2024 by ReadersMagnet, LLC. All rights reserved.

Cover design by Jhiee Oraiz
Interior design by Daniel Lopez

# A JOURNEY THROUGH LIFE

YVONNE BRONSTORPH

ReadersMagnet, LLC

## CONTENTS

A Journey Through Life . . . . . . . . . . . . . . . . . . . . . . . . . . . . . . . 1
A Precious Gift . . . . . . . . . . . . . . . . . . . . . . . . . . . . . . . . . . . . . . 2
America Arise . . . . . . . . . . . . . . . . . . . . . . . . . . . . . . . . . . . . . . 3
Autumn . . . . . . . . . . . . . . . . . . . . . . . . . . . . . . . . . . . . . . . . . . . 5
Days of Youthfulness . . . . . . . . . . . . . . . . . . . . . . . . . . . . . . . . 6
Doves . . . . . . . . . . . . . . . . . . . . . . . . . . . . . . . . . . . . . . . . . . . . . 7
Friends . . . . . . . . . . . . . . . . . . . . . . . . . . . . . . . . . . . . . . . . . . . . 8
God is Real . . . . . . . . . . . . . . . . . . . . . . . . . . . . . . . . . . . . . . . . 9
Grief . . . . . . . . . . . . . . . . . . . . . . . . . . . . . . . . . . . . . . . . . . . . . 10
Inspiration . . . . . . . . . . . . . . . . . . . . . . . . . . . . . . . . . . . . . . . . 11
Lest We Forget . . . . . . . . . . . . . . . . . . . . . . . . . . . . . . . . . . . . 13
Love is Forever . . . . . . . . . . . . . . . . . . . . . . . . . . . . . . . . . . . . 15
Love . . . . . . . . . . . . . . . . . . . . . . . . . . . . . . . . . . . . . . . . . . . . . 16
Morning . . . . . . . . . . . . . . . . . . . . . . . . . . . . . . . . . . . . . . . . . 17
Mother . . . . . . . . . . . . . . . . . . . . . . . . . . . . . . . . . . . . . . . . . . 18
Mountains . . . . . . . . . . . . . . . . . . . . . . . . . . . . . . . . . . . . . . . 19
My Dream . . . . . . . . . . . . . . . . . . . . . . . . . . . . . . . . . . . . . . . 20
My Island Home . . . . . . . . . . . . . . . . . . . . . . . . . . . . . . . . . . 21
Run Silent, Run . . . . . . . . . . . . . . . . . . . . . . . . . . . . . . . . . . . 23
Spring . . . . . . . . . . . . . . . . . . . . . . . . . . . . . . . . . . . . . . . . . . . 24
Tropical Sunset . . . . . . . . . . . . . . . . . . . . . . . . . . . . . . . . . . . 25
We Saw Them Fall . . . . . . . . . . . . . . . . . . . . . . . . . . . . . . . . 26

# A JOURNEY THROUGH LIFE

As we journey through life we experience many emotions. In these poems, I have shared my heart-felt emotions for the beauty and wonder of God's creation and love, joy, grief, a mother's love and my longing for the sun-drenched vibrant colors of my island home and many other sentiments. I hope you will enjoy this walk with me.

# A PRECIOUS GIFT

God smiled as He blessed us with a beautiful baby
Eyes looking up at us bright, shiny, black as diamonds,
Tiny mouth the picture of a pink rosebud,
Little elfin ears with star-like points,
Sharlene, our bonny little girl.

Shiny eyes to Daddy, Rosebud to Mummy,
We gazed at this little person,
Her face glowing with smiles, a picture of serenity,
Together we drank her in with eyes of love,
Sharlene our darling, God's masterpiece.

Through the years, God has molded her into a young lady,
Beautiful, full of swan-like grace,
Caring, loving, tender-hearted,
Spirited as a steed, nurturing, quick-witted,
Overcoming challenges, rising above dashed dreams,
Knowing that Jesus holds her close to His bosom
Guiding her with love along life's path,
Sharlene a child of God.

# AMERICA ARISE

America has arisen above its history
Writing new pages into the annals,
This great country, champion of nations,
Leader of freedom and democracy
Has stood the test of time.

America stands a bastion of change
Proving the struggles and dreams were not in vain,
For what many thought impossible
Is now at last a reality
The voice of its citizens have spoken.
Come one, come all

Stand firm for the good of this mighty land,
Let us not ever be divided,
Duty demands we proudly stand
As one in such a blessed land.

So let the church bells ring
Across mountains and vales,
Let people rejoice and dance in the streets
And voice burst forth in song
While marching bands play to and fro.

Star-spangled banners wave in the breeze
Eagles soar without-stretched wings,
America the giant has woken from her sleep
A new day dawns over the land in the east.
Arise America rise!

# AUTUMN

Autumn quietly enters in all mellowness
Mountain trails prettied with yellow and orange trees;
Fabulous vibrant hues from which eyes cannot rest,
A spectacular display of nature at its best.

Golden wheat fields stretch in never-ending lines,
Pumpkin patches splashed with orange colors,
Open meadows arrayed in reds - spotted with green
Charming hamlets and rolling hills paint a scenic vista.

Watching leaves turn color and fall from trees,
Maples, oaks, aspens, and hickories
Wearing crimson, russet and brilliant scarlet coats,
The elms, dogwoods and tupelos too
A vivid palette of reds, oranges and browns.

Season for reaping the ripened crops
And celebrate bounteous harvests of the land,
An extravagant display like no other,
Nature's one last blast of color,
Before settling into winter's slumber.

## DAYS OF YOUTHFULNESS

They come to us, the innocent ones
Their thoughts and hopes unfettered,
The world a vision of all possibilities
Thinking with immortal souls
Being too young to die.

They come to us, bubbling over with life
The spring of a deer in their steps,
Heads defiantly tossed, eyes aglow,
Sparkling, trusting, laughing, warm
There are the days of their youth.

They come to us, minds to be molded
Dreams yet to be dreamed,
Energy raw, unharnessed, untamed,
Running, playing, free as the wind
Gods little children, our future.

They come to us, spirits to be guided
Hearts made happy with songs,
Till some sublime day not far away
There emerges diamond in all its brilliance,
As days of youthfulness are laid to rest.

# DOVES

Soaring through the air so rare
Rising to meet azure blue sky,
A symbol of peace I am
Since by Noah's hand set free.

Weddings I visit oftentimes
Perched atop white tiered cakes,
Sitting swan-like on many layers
Sugar-coated, sweet to taste.

Magicians pull me from their hats
Delighting children with eyes agog,
Tricks I know, oh so well
Cuddled in some pocket fold.

Freely I was born to fly
Gliding, rising, floating, wings outstretched,
My fronded feathers you will never tame
For I was born to soar above.

# FRIENDS

In life's journey God provides friends
Who give us hope and cheer each day,
To lift our spirits when thoughts are dire
And make us laugh when we want to cry.

Friends, to lend kind ears when hearts are troubled
Or say I care with just a smile,
Telling us all is well not to worry
When in waters deep we tread.

Playing happy childhood games
Running carefree through the fields,
Sharing silly, giddy, blushing dreams,
Friends forever we gladly pledged.

# GOD IS REAL

My God is real,
He wakes me each morning
To enjoy the beauty of His Creation
And spend my days in His Divine presence.

The trees are not just trees to me,
They came from the same Creator's hand
I feel an affinity to them all,
As leaves whisper "we are surely one".

My God fashioned and painted the flowers,
Lilies dressed in tutus white, corals and pinks,
Heavenly perfumes rising from delicate rose
Exotic orchids, lavender or white are His too.

He molded the little red robin and sparrow
The great soaring eagle and graceful swan,
Do they worry about today or tomorrow?
No, God lovingly tends their bands.

Look! He is everywhere
Whether skies so blue or oceans wide,
Brilliant sun or silvery moon
I truly know my God is real.

# GRIEF

When your heart is full of grief
Days are long and nights dreary,
And you grow saddened and weary
Reflect on times spent in laughter together.

Tears are difficult to keep at bay
Your loving voice I want to hear,
Smiling face that brings me cheer
Melodic laughter ringing through the air.

I ponder the happy hours we shared
The many times you held my hand,
Sitting, holding audience with everyone,
Imparting wisdom from a life blessed and long.

Will this pain in me ever cease?
Which unkind hand has plucked my heart,
Crushed it, shredded it, crumpled it,
Then threw it bleeding away.

Time with its ever fleeting wings,
Someday with balm will beckon to my heart,
The season of healing has come at last
And I can live, despite that piece you will forever hold.

# INSPIRATION

Love yourself!
You will succeed and you will never walk alone.
You were created for a purpose in this life –
To love and be loved,
Happy and be made happy,
Full of joy and be joyful,
Protect and be protected,
Respect and be respected,
Dream and be dreamed about.

Walk tall and be esteemed,
See beauty and be beautiful, for true beauty
Is in the heart, and not only the face.
Life is full of many challenges, surprises and pitfalls,
Find that hidden courage within, release it
Reach for the stars and soar with the eagles.

But as you step from this phase to that of adulthood
And its responsibilities:
Set your eyes on your chosen prize,
Stand steadfast and firm.
Let no one deter you from the course you have set,
Rise above the difficult situations,
Remember! Each day is an education.

Grasp every opportunity before you,
Conquer fear, you are a winner:
Time waits for no one,
Hold your head high,
Experience the joy of living.

## LEST WE FORGET

Our men and women bravely serve,
Bastions of courage faithful to the end,
Battling to protect our blessed land,
Laying down their precious lives without thought,
For the sake of mankind's nature-given right to liberty,
God will not forget them!

Hearts undaunted and youthful boldness,
Ever ready to answer the call to arms,
On rugged land, raging seas, or never ending blue skies,
Battle readied, combat geared, tanks rumbling,
Camouflaged, sanded, muddied and bloodied.
Never shall we forget them!

Valiant, fearless, gallant, audacious,
Booted footsteps trod on foreign soils.
Rushing headlong to the plaintive cries,
Of earth's tortured, oppressed, forgotten,
Denied every right to justice,
Forget them not!

Homecoming for some is in Glory,
Others - shattered lives and dreams forever changed,
Limbs missing, minds and hearts broken,
Grieving mothers, wives, fathers, children
Sacrifices made for the freedom cry,
Let us always remember them!

Heroes all, lest we forget,
Sung or unsung, known or unknown,
Honored or silent, willing or unwilling,
Names eternally etched in our memories,
Framed smiling faces not flag draped caskets,
Looking into God's radiant face
We will remember them!

# LOVE IS FOREVER

*For Alexis*

On day in May you walked into my life,
Just an ordinary day, two ordinary people,
Our hands touched, but for a moment,
Two hearts were entwined forever.

Our love was born to last, a love like no other,
Pure, warm, azure as the deepest ocean,
Clear as the bluest sky on a sunny day,
Love – solid, planted as the rock of all ages,
Unmoving as the golden sunrise in the morn.

Where did you learn to love with such passion!
Or give of yourself so completely, unheeding your inner being,
Has no one told you, or do you not know,
Man's love is an emotion apart from his life!

When the night is still, I sit alone with my thoughts,
To ponder this sudden, warm all-consuming fire,
Which touches the very fiber of my being,
Allowing myself to bask in this love-cocoon,
For I know that this love will last forever.

# LOVE

Love, what are you?
The theme of movies and stories,
Essence of poems, songs,
Are there words to describe you?

Love shrouded in mystery,
For some you are a season,
Yet for others you last a lifetime,
Are you just a fantasy?

Lovers live to hold you dear,
Others kill to keep you near,
Some never know you are there,
Do you really care?

# MORNING

Night quietly creeps away,
Making sure there's another day,
Sun wakes brightly in the east,
Nudging every man, bird and beast.

Morning breaks forth with its sun,
A busy day has once more begun.
Diamond dewdrops dot the grass,
Drowsy world can stir at last.

Buttercups open to the waiting bees,
Giving sweet nectar with no fees,
Morning glories waiting in the wings,
In purples and blues to dance and sing.

Gilded morning praises your God,
Happy skylarks give Him a nod,
Before you slip into cluttered day,
For surely He will direct the way.

# MOTHER

When I debuted into life it was you and I,
In that merry month of flowering May,
Daughter to a mother ever so mild,
With a countenance so sweet and kind.

Your hugs and kisses were never far away,
Gentle hands to soothe every hurt and pain,
Tears were few because of you,
Contentment and laughter you taught me too.

Healing hands that delicately smocked my dresses,
Fashioned lacy doilies, slips and covers,
Filling my room with frills, lace and ribbons,
A beautiful bower bedecked for your princess.

To me you were perfect in every way,
Smiles never left your pretty face,
Never did words of anger between us pass,
As in dreams and hopes you cheered me on.

God blessed me with you for many years,
Knowing dear mother how much I needed you,
But as I watched you quietly slip into His arms,
Again it was just you and I.

## MOUNTAINS

The mountains rise majestic astride the earth,
Capped with ice or verdant grass,
Stretching upwards to the sky,
Scarred, craggy, grooved or smooth,
Sculptured by the Creator's hand.

Man looks up and see, not a mountain,
But a challenge to his very nature,
He was created to rule over the mountains,
Not cower at their feet,
For he too, was fashioned by God's hand.

Yet the mountains tower over the land,
Blue mountains veiled by morning mists,
Green mountains washed by rain from above,
Pink mountains painted by the sunset,
White mountains capped by frozen snow.

From rolling hills to mighty Everest,
Whether grumbling deep or spewing lava in the air,
Or aglow with fire's consuming coat,
Lofty, peaked in grandeur you still stand,
Never to be moved by man's chiseling hands.

## MY DREAM

You Lord, are my dream come through
Just my knowing with you
May I live each day
Desiring only to be with you.

A love so pure and so perfect
Freely given and complete,
Love that knows no bounds
Asking for nothing in return.

Walking in the valleys
You hold my hand
Troubled thoughts You say - I understand
Tearing eyes - You dry with only a song.

Running on mountain tops - You are there
Celebrating salvation - You whisper in my ear
Greater am I than your wildest dreams
Loving you before time ever was.

# MY ISLAND HOME

A jewel in the sea,
Is this beautiful isle,
Rising from sandy shores,
To peaks of mountains blue,
Jamaica, Land I love.

White sands dotted with fringed palms,
Almond trees spreading heavy branches,
Turquoise waters in greens and blues,
Gently, softly lapping sunny beaches,
Jamaica. Isle of beauty.

Land where the Poinciana's grow,
Their layered branches splattered with brilliant reds,
Lush lignum vitae with roots firmly planted,
Lavender petals peeping through leaves,
Jamaica, Caribbean pearl.

Golden poui, a splash of yellow hanging leafless,
Bird of paradise blossoms kissing garden walls,
Ginger lilies sporting scarlet and pink dresses,
Visions of color like the rainbow,
Jamaica, another Eden.

Land of wood and water you are called,
Rivers running in deep gorges, quietly washing slated stones,
Icy cool, crispy fresh, glassy clear,
Realm strewn with trees, hedges, copses running wild,
Jamaica, God's creation.

My eyes close and I see this island home,
A gallery of painted scenes framing my wall,
I see the flowers and inhale their fragrance,
Hands trail through sparkling waters,
As my mind tiptoes through memories past,
Jamaica, ever my island home.

# RUN SILENT, RUN

Rivers run silently through the land,
Carving serpentine shapes in the earth,
Supplying crystalline water to this orb,
Life - support so vital to man and beast.

Civilizations around you spawned,
Rising and spreading from muddy shores,
Key to man's enlightened path,
Merging cultures far away.

High on the mountain slopes you spring,
Gentle trickle to scurrying over stones,
Swift flowing stream sprinting along your course,
Till a mighty rushing river, you become.

Raging water that sweep grand abodes,
Tumbling, roaring torrent gone wild,
Crushing bridges, edifices, giant trees in your path,
Are you Mother Nature's angry bath?

Your power challenges man's very being,
Churning, roiling, tossing waters he must conquer,
Deep solemn gorges beckoning that inquisitive spirit,
Babbling, bubbling, rippling brook,
Silty, slippery, sloshy banks he must meander.

# SPRING

Spring emerges discarding winter's dreary cloak,
Time for daffodils to wake and bloom,
Fields of golden flowers waving in the breeze,
Sweet violets symbol of fertility and love,
Sprinkled atop the greening grass.

Beloved azaleas in varied shades of pink,
Neatly hedged-rowed or shrubbery abloom,
Miniatured alyssum in yellow and white,
Cascading over rocks and overlaying mossy ground,
Poppies orange and red stand opened to the sun.

Splayed dogwood branches festooned white with flowers,
Lush magnolias with creamy blooms and silver-backed leaves,
Their sweet lemon fragrances filling the air,
Luxuriant cherry blossoms marching in rows,
Tulip, irises, freesias, peonies, budding everywhere,
Till spring with all grace, curtsies to summer's heat.

# TROPICAL SUNSET

Trades wind are wafting over the land,
As the cool of the evening nudges at the heat,
The pace of the working has gradually ceased,
The sun glides ever swifter to the west.

Gathering her golden skirts of chiffon,
She begins her silent descent to the sea,
Opening paints, her masterpiece takes to the sky,
In shades of gold and orange you can never imagine.

Bands of vermillion, saffron, orange, peach,
Amber, coral, apricot, maize,
Stretch in endless lines across the horizon,
While dusts of fluffy clouds tiptoe, to and fro.

Still as the sun silently slips,
Gracefully this rich plethora of color glides too,
Then pausing - with one last burst of brilliant glow,
She collects her richly painted canvas,
Slides gently into the waiting sea, and is no more.

# WE SAW THEM FALL

A clear blue sky canopied the city,
Mother Earth wore her sunniest dress,
And tall majestic buildings outlined the skyline,
Like fingers outstretched to heaven.

The Towers rose loftily above all else,
A celebration of man's creative genius,
Like sunflowers astride a field of daises,
Fashioned by God's hand,
And we say we saw them fall.

Offices buzz with life, phones ringing,
People talking, laughing, working,
For this day has begun like any other,
Unknowing of the evil winging its way,
Through the cool morning air.
Like a sudden clash of thunder, a day of infamy is born,
We watch in horror as one of man's wonders,
Becomes man's ultimate weapon of destruction.
Smoke - black, gray, erupts in the air,
Innocent souls are carried into eternity – forever!
As we see them fall.

The rest of the world looks on aghast!
Hearts pound, stomach churn, and eyes weep,
For America has lost its innocence,
People run to and fro, D-Day is visiting the shores of our homeland,
O! Why must we watch them fall.

Our minds cannot understand why?
As numbness envelops our every nerve,
And all our childhood nightmares – frightening,
Chilling, come rushing to meet us.
As we are seeing them fall.
We feel every emotion, except joy or peace,

We feel guilty for being alive,
The only thought that stays our sanity,
Is the God in whom we believe, trust and have faith,
Yet we lift our eyes heavenward and say, "Why, Father, why?"
Why did they have to fall?

We watch our bravest – firefighter, police and unknowing heroes,
Rushing to help: there are lives to save,
People to be rescued: for that is what they do!
They walk purposefully into the smoking Towers,
Never to return again,
They fall!

For man's steel has buckled under man's wonder,
As gray dust furls upwards,
And the majestic Towers are no more,
With bated breath we watch, both man and mortar are just a memory,
We saw them fall.

Who will comfort the wives, husbands, sons, daughters, mothers, fathers,
Children crying for mothers' arms which will never hold them or voices hear,
Who will explain this wanton destruction?
And tell America her freedom is violated.
For we saw them fall.

The time for healing will come,
Tears will never stop or the pain go away,
But one day God will tell us why we saw them fall,
Until that day we will remember,
We saw them fall.

www.ingramcontent.com/pod-product-compliance
Lightning Source LLC
LaVergne TN
LVHW010421070526
838199LV00064B/5371